love
your
body

ALSO BY LOUISE HAY

Forgiveness/Loving the Inner Child
How to Love Yourself
Meditations for Personal Healing
Meditations to Heal Your Life (audio book)
Morning and Evening Meditations
101 Power Thoughts
Overcoming Fears
The Power Is Within You (audio book)
The Power of Your Spoken Word
Receiving Prosperity
Self-Esteem Affirmations (subliminal)
Self-Healing
Stress-Free (subliminal)
Totality of Possibilities
What I Believe and Deep Relaxation
You Can Heal Your Life (audio book)
You Can Heal Your Life Study Course
Your Thoughts Create Your Life

DVDs
Receiving Prosperity
You Can Heal Your Life Study Course
You Can Heal Your Life, THE MOVIE (also available in an expanded edition)
You Can Trust Your Life (with Cheryl Richardson)

CARD DECKS
Healthy Body Cards
I Can Do It® Cards
*I Can Do It® Cards . . . for Creativity, Forgiveness,
Health, Job Success, Wealth, Romance*
Power Thought Cards
Power Thoughts for Teens
Power Thought Sticky Cards
Wisdom Cards

CALENDAR
I Can Do It® Calendar (for each individual year)

and

THE ESSENTIAL LOUISE HAY COLLECTION
(comprising *You Can Heal Your Life, Heal Your Body,* and
The Power Is Within You in a single volume)

❖

love your body

**A POSITIVE AFFIRMATION GUIDE FOR
LOVING AND APPRECIATING YOUR BODY**

Louise Hay

HAY HOUSE, INC.
Carlsbad, California • New York City
London • Sydney • Johannesburg
Vancouver • Hong Kong • New Delhi

Published and distributed in the United States by: Hay House, Inc.:
www.hayhouse.com® • *Published and distributed in Australia by:* Hay
House Australia Pty. Ltd.: www.hayhouse.com.au • *Published and distributed in the United Kingdom by:* Hay House UK, Ltd.: www.hayhouse
.co.uk • *Published and distributed in the Republic of South Africa by:*
Hay House SA (Pty), Ltd.: www.hayhouse.co.za • *Distributed in Canada
by:* Raincoast Books: www.raincoast.com • *Published in India by:* Hay
House Publishers India: www.hayhouse.co.in

Designed by: Tricia Breidenthal • *Edited by:* Jill Kramer

Library of Congress Catalog Card No.: 89-84644

ISBN: 978-1-56170-602-0

1st edition *(I Love My Body)*, March 1985
1st digital printing, April 2015

Printed in the United States of America

*To all the bodies on the planet,
I dedicate this offering with love.*

Contents

affirmations
for a
healthy body

Little babies love every inch of their bodies. They have no guilt, no shame, and no comparison. You were like that, and then somewhere along the line you listened to others who told you that you were "not good enough." You began to criticize your body, thinking perhaps that that's where your flaws were.

Let's drop all that nonsense and get back to loving our bodies and accepting them totally as they are. Of course they will change—and if we give our bodies love, they will change for the better.

The subconscious mind has no sense of humor and does not know false from true. It only accepts what we say and what we think as the material from which it builds. By repeating these positive affirmations over and over, you will be planting new seeds in the fertile soil of your subconscious mind, and they will become true for you.

Stand in front of a mirror and repeat each affirmation treatment (new thought pattern) ten times. Do this twice a day. Also write the affirmations ten times sometime during the day. Work with one treatment a day until you have gone through the whole book. You can use the blank pages to write your own positive affirmations. Then, if there is any part of your body you still dislike or have a problem with, use that particular treatment daily for at least a month, or until positive change takes place.

If doubts or fears or negative thoughts come up, just recognize them for what they are—old limiting beliefs that want to stay around. They have no power over you. Say to them gently, "Out! I no longer need you." Then repeat your affirmations again.

Where you stop working is where your resistance is. Notice the part of your body that you don't want to love. Give this part extra attention so you may go beyond the limitation. Release the resistance.

In this way, within a short time, you will have a body you really love. And your body will respond by giving you excellent health. Each part of your body will be working perfectly as a harmonious whole.

You will even find lines disappearing, weight normalizing, and posture straightening.

That which we constantly affirm becomes true for us.

PERSONAL NOTES ✤ AFFIRMATIONS

i love my mind

My mind enables me to recognize the beautiful Miracle of my Body. I am glad to be alive. I affirm with my mind that I have the power to heal myself. My mind chooses the thoughts that create my future moment by moment. My power comes through the use of my mind. I choose thoughts that make me feel good. I love and appreciate my beautiful mind!

PERSONAL NOTES ✣ AFFIRMATIONS

i love my scalp

My scalp is relaxed and peaceful. It is loose and easy. It provides a nourished bed for my hair. My hair is able to grow freely and luxuriously. I choose the thoughts that massage my scalp with love. I love and appreciate my beautiful scalp!

PERSONAL NOTES ✛ AFFIRMATIONS

i love my hair

I trust the process of life to take care of my every need, and I grow strong and peaceful. I relax my scalp and give my beautiful hair room to grow luxuriously. I lovingly groom my hair and choose the thoughts that support its growth and strength. I love and appreciate my beautiful hair!

PERSONAL NOTES ✤ AFFIRMATIONS

i love my eyes

I have perfect vision. I see clearly in every direction. I see with love my past, my present, and my future. My mind chooses the way I look at life. I see with new eyes. I see good in everyone and everywhere. I now lovingly create the life I love to look at. I love and appreciate my beautiful eyes!

PERSONAL NOTES ✣ AFFIRMATIONS

i love my ears

I am balanced and poised and one with all of life. I choose the thoughts that create harmony around me. I listen with love to the good and the pleasant. I hear the cry for love that is hidden in everyone's message. I am willing to understand others, and I have compassion for them. I rejoice in my ability to hear life. I have a receptive capacity of mind. I am willing to hear. I love and appreciate my beautiful ears!

PERSONAL NOTES ✛ AFFIRMATIONS

i love my nose

I am at peace with everyone around me. No person, place, or thing has any power over me. I am the power and authority in my world. I choose the thoughts that recognize my own true worth. I recognize my own intuitive ability. I trust my intuition, for I am always in contact with Universal Wisdom and Truth. I always go in the right direction for me. I love and appreciate my beautiful nose!

PERSONAL NOTES ✣ AFFIRMATIONS

i love my mouth

I nourish myself by taking in new ideas. I prepare new concepts for digestion and assimilation. I make decisions with ease based upon the principles of Truth. I have a good taste for life. I choose the thoughts that enable me to speak with love. I speak up for myself, secure in my own true worth. I love and appreciate my beautiful mouth!

PERSONAL NOTES ✣ AFFIRMATIONS

i love my teeth

My teeth are strong and healthy. I bite into life with joy. I thoughtfully and completely chew all my experiences. I am a decisive person. I make decisions with ease, and I stick to them. I choose the thoughts that create a solid inner foundation. I trust my Inner Wisdom, knowing that I will always choose what is best for me at any given moment. I love and appreciate my beautiful teeth!

PERSONAL NOTES ❖ AFFIRMATIONS

i love my gums

My gums are the picture of health. They support and protect my teeth with love. It is easy for me to stick to my decisions. I back up my decisions with spiritual convictions. I am strongly centered in Wisdom and Truth. I choose the thoughts that create only right action in my life. I love and appreciate my beautiful gums!

i love my voice

I voice my opinions. I speak up for myself. I sing the praises of love and joy. My words are the music of life. I choose the thoughts that express beauty and gratitude. I proclaim my oneness with all of life. I love and appreciate my beautiful voice!

i love my neck

I willingly turn to acknowledge other viewpoints and other ways of doing things. I am free to acknowledge it all. I am willing to change. I choose the thoughts that keep me flexible in my ideas and in my creative expression. I express myself freely and joyously. I am safe. I love and appreciate my beautiful neck!

PERSONAL NOTES ✤ AFFIRMATIONS

i love my throat

My throat is my avenue of expression and creativity. I keep it open and free. I sing with great joy. I choose the thoughts that allow me to express my creativity. I lovingly declare to the world my self-worth and my self-esteem. I love and appreciate my beautiful throat.

PERSONAL NOTES ✣ AFFIRMATIONS

i love my shoulders

I shoulder my responsibilities with ease. My burdens are light—like feathers in the wind. I stand tall and free, and I joyfully carry my experiences. My shoulders are beautiful and straight and strong. I choose the thoughts that make my way easy and free. Love releases and relaxes. I love my life. I love and appreciate my beautiful shoulders!

PERSONAL NOTES ❖ AFFIRMATIONS

i love my breasts

My breasts are the perfect size and shape for my body. They are healthy and will always be healthy. I always nourish and take care of myself before I take care of others. I choose the thoughts that nurture me in every way. I love and appreciate my beautiful breasts.

PERSONAL NOTES ✤ AFFIRMATIONS

i love my arms

I am protective of myself and my loved ones. I welcome life with joy. I have great ability to embrace life's experiences. My capacity for the enjoyment of life is enormous. I choose the thoughts that enable me to accept change easily and move in any direction. I am strong and able and capable at all times. I love and appreciate my beautiful arms!

i love my wrists

My wrists are flexible and free. It is with ease that I accept pleasure into my life. I deserve all the good that I receive. I choose the thoughts that make it easy for me to enjoy all that I have. I love and appreciate my beautiful wrists!

i love my hands

My hands are free to hold life in any way they wish. My hands have endless ways of handling events and people. I choose the thoughts that handle my experiences with joy and ease. Each detail is taken care of in Divine Right Order. I handle life with love; therefore, I am secure, I am safe, I am myself. I am at peace. I love and appreciate my beautiful hands!

PERSONAL NOTES ✛ AFFIRMATIONS

i love my fingers

My fingers give me much pleasure. I love my ability to touch and feel, to probe and inspect, to mend and repair, to create, and to fashion with love. I put my finger on the pulse of life; and I am in tune with every person, place, and thing. I choose the thoughts that enable me to touch with love. I love and appreciate my beautiful fingers!

PERSONAL NOTES ✣ AFFIRMATIONS

i love my fingernails

My fingernails are a joy to look at. I am protected and safe. As I relax and trust life to unfold before me, my nails grow strong and hard. I love and appreciate all the wonderful details of my life. I choose the thoughts that let the minor details be handled easily and effortlessly. I love and appreciate my beautiful fingernails!

i love my spine

My spine is a place of harmony and love. Each vertebra is lovingly connected to its neighbors. There is perfect, smooth interaction between them all. This makes me strong, yet flexible. I can reach to the heavens and bend to the earth. I choose the thoughts that keep me safe and free. I love and appreciate my beautiful spine!

PERSONAL NOTES ✣ AFFIRMATIONS

i love my back

I am supported by life itself. I feel emotionally supported. I release all fears. I feel loved. I release the past and all past experiences. I let go of that which is in back of me. I now trust the process of life. I choose the thoughts that supply all my needs. Life prospers me in expected and unexpected ways. I know that life is for me. I stand straight and tall, supported by the love of life. I love and appreciate my beautiful back!

PERSONAL NOTES ✛ AFFIRMATIONS

i love my flexibility

God has given me the ability to be flexible and to flow with life like a willow tree. I can bend and stretch and always come back to my center. I choose the thoughts that strengthen this ability to be supple and pliant. I love and appreciate my beautiful flexibility!

PERSONAL NOTES ✣ AFFIRMATIONS

i love my chest

I take in and give out nourishment in perfect balance. Life supplies everything I need. I am free to be me, and I allow others the freedom to be who they are. Life protects us all. It is safe for all of us to grow up. I nourish only with love. I choose the thoughts that create freedom for us all. I love and appreciate my beautiful chest!

PERSONAL NOTES ✣ AFFIRMATIONS

i love my lungs

I have a right to take up space. I have a right to exist. I take in and give out life fully and freely. It is safe to take in my environment. I trust the Power that supplies my breath in such great abundance. There is enough breath to last as long as I shall choose to live. There is enough life and sustenance to last for as long as I shall choose to live. I now choose the thoughts that create safety for me. I love and appreciate my beautiful lungs!

PERSONAL NOTES ✤ AFFIRMATIONS

i love my breath

My breath is so precious to me. It is a treasure and a life-giving substance. I know it is safe for me to live. I love life. I breathe in life deeply and fully. I breathe in and out in perfect harmony. I choose the thoughts that create a loving and sweet breath. I am a joy to be around. I flow with the breath of life. I love and appreciate my beautiful breath!

PERSONAL NOTES ✣ AFFIRMATIONS

i love my glands

My glands are the starting points for my self-expression. My self-expression is my own unique approach to life. I am a unique individual. I respect my individuality. I originate in the depth of my being all the good I find unfolding in my life. My originality begins with the thoughts I choose to think. My spiritual immunity and strength are strong and balanced. I am a go-getter. I have "get-up-and-go." I love and appreciate my beautiful glands!

PERSONAL NOTES ✢ AFFIRMATIONS

i love my heart

My heart lovingly carries joy throughout my body, nourishing the cells. Joyous new ideas are now circulating freely within me. I am the joy of life, expressing and receiving. I now choose the thoughts that create an ever-joyous now. It is safe to be alive at every age. I radiate love in every direction, and my whole life is a joy. I love with my heart. I love and appreciate my beautiful heart!

PERSONAL NOTES ✛ AFFIRMATIONS

i love my blood

The blood in my veins is pure joy. This joy of life flows freely throughout my body. I am living with joy and happiness. I choose the thoughts that create enthusiasm for life. My life is rich and full and joyous. I love and appreciate my beautiful blood!

PERSONAL NOTES ✛ AFFIRMATIONS

i love my nerves

I have a wondrous nervous system. My nerves enable me to communicate with all of life. I can sense and feel and understand on very deep levels. I feel safe and secure. My nerves are allowed to relax peacefully. I choose the thoughts that bring me peace. I love and appreciate my beautiful nerves!

PERSONAL NOTES ✜ AFFIRMATIONS

i love my stomach

It is with joy that I digest the experiences of life. Life agrees with me. I easily assimilate each new moment of every day. All is well in my world. I choose the thoughts that glorify my being. I trust life to feed me that which I need. I know my self-worth. I am good enough just as I am. I am a Divine, Magnificent Expression of Life. I assimilate this thought and make it true for me. I love and appreciate my beautiful stomach!

PERSONAL NOTES ✛ AFFIRMATIONS

i love my liver

I let go of everything I no longer need. I joyfully release all irritation, criticism, and condemnation. My consciousness is now cleansed and healed. Everything in my life is in Divine Right Order. Everything that happens is for my highest good and greatest joy. I find love everywhere in my life. I choose the thoughts that heal, cleanse, and uplift me. I love and appreciate my beautiful liver!

PERSONAL NOTES ✣ AFFIRMATIONS

i love my kidneys

It is safe for me to grow up and to accept the life I have created. I release the old and welcome the new. My kidneys efficiently eliminate the old poisons of my mind. I now choose the thoughts that create my world; therefore, I accept everything in my world as perfect. My emotions are stabilized in love. I love and appreciate my beautiful kidneys!

PERSONAL NOTES ✣ AFFIRMATIONS

i love my spleen

My only obsession is with the joy of life. My true identity is one of peace and love and joy. I choose the thoughts that create joy for me in every area of my life. My spleen is healthy and happy and normal. I am safe. I choose to experience the sweetness of life. I love and appreciate my beautiful spleen!

PERSONAL NOTES ✣ AFFIRMATIONS

i love my immune system

My immune system is strong and vigorous. It protects my body and keeps me in perfect health. Knowing that my immune system responds to my every thought, I choose healthy thinking. I think only loving, positive thoughts that enhance and support my immune system. I love and appreciate my beautiful immune system.

i love my waistline

I have a beautiful waistline. It is normal and natural and very flexible. I can bend and twist in every direction. I choose the thoughts that allow me to enjoy exercise in a form that is pleasing to me. My waistline is the perfect size for me. I love and appreciate my beautiful waistline!

PERSONAL NOTES ✛ AFFIRMATIONS

i love my hips

I carry myself through life in perfect balance. There is always something new I am moving toward. Every age has its interests and goals. I choose the thoughts that keep my hips firm and powerful. I am powerful at the very seat of my life. I love and appreciate my beautiful hips!

PERSONAL NOTES ✣ AFFIRMATIONS

i love my buttocks

My buttocks grow more beautiful every day. They are the seat of my power. I know I am a powerful being. I recognize and accept my power. I choose the thoughts that enable me to use my power lovingly and wisely. It feels wonderful to be powerful. I love and appreciate my beautiful buttocks!

PERSONAL NOTES ✢ AFFIRMATIONS

i love my colon

I am an open channel for good to flow in and through me—freely, generously, and joyfully. I willingly release all thoughts and things that clutter or clog. All is normal, harmonious, and perfect in my life. I live only in the ever-present now. I choose the thoughts that keep me open and receptive to the flow of life. I have perfect intake, assimilation, and elimination. I love and appreciate my beautiful colon!

PERSONAL NOTES ✣ AFFIRMATIONS

i love my bladder

I am at peace with my thoughts and emotions. I am at peace with those around me. No person, place, or thing has any power over me, for I am the only thinker in my mind. I choose the thoughts that keep me serene. I willingly and lovingly release old concepts and ideas. They flow out of me easily and joyously. I love and appreciate my beautiful bladder!

i love my genitals

I rejoice in my sexuality. It is normal and natural and perfect for me. My genitals are beautiful and normal and natural and perfect for me. I am good enough and beautiful enough exactly as I am, right here and right now. I appreciate the pleasure my body gives me. It is safe for me to enjoy my body. I choose the thoughts that allow me to love and appreciate my beautiful genitals!

PERSONAL NOTES ✣ AFFIRMATIONS

i love my rectum

I see the beauty of my body in every cell and in every organ. My rectum is as normal and natural and beautiful as any other part of my body. I am totally accepting of each function of my body and rejoice in its efficiency and perfection. My heart and my rectum and my eyes and my toes are all equally important and beautiful. I choose the thoughts that allow me to accept with love every part of my body. I love and appreciate my beautiful rectum!

PERSONAL NOTES ✜ AFFIRMATIONS

i love my legs

I now choose to release all old childhood hurts and pains. I refuse to live in the past. I am a now person living in today. As I forgive and release the past, my thighs become firm and beautiful. I have total mobility to move in any direction. I move forward in life, unencumbered by the past. My calf muscles are relaxed and strong. I choose the thoughts that allow me to move forward with joy. I love and appreciate my beautiful legs!

i love my knees

I am flexible and flowing. I am giving and forgiving. I bend and flow with ease. I have understanding and compassion, and I easily forgive the past and everyone in it. I acknowledge others and praise them at every turn. I choose the thoughts that keep me open and receptive to the love and joy that is flowing freely everywhere. I kneel at the altar of myself. I love and appreciate my beautiful knees!

i love my ankles

My ankles give me mobility and direction. I release all fear and guilt. I accept pleasure with ease. I move in the direction of my highest good. I choose the thoughts that bring pleasure and joy into my life. I am flexible and flowing. I love and appreciate my beautiful ankles!

PERSONAL NOTES ✣ AFFIRMATIONS

i love my feet

I have such wonderful understanding. I stand firmly rooted in the Truth. My understanding of myself and of others and of life is constantly growing. I am nourished by Mother Earth, and the Universal Intelligence teaches me all I need to know. I walk upon this planet safe and secure, moving forward toward my greater good. I move with ease through time and space. I choose the thoughts that create a wonderful future, and I move into it. I love and appreciate my beautiful feet!

PERSONAL NOTES ✤ AFFIRMATIONS

i love my toes

My toes are inspectors of the future, going before me to clear the way. They are straight, flexible, and strong. They reach out, feeling and finding the perfect pathway in life. I choose the thoughts that protect my pathway. As I move forward, all details take care of themselves. I love and appreciate my beautiful toes!

PERSONAL NOTES ✢ AFFIRMATIONS

i love my bones

I am strong and sound. I am well structured and balanced. My bones support me and love me. Every bone is important to me. I choose the thoughts that strengthen my life. I am composed of the materials of the Universe. I am one with the structure of life. I love and appreciate my beautiful bones!

PERSONAL NOTES ✜ AFFIRMATIONS

i love my muscles

My muscles give me the ability to move in my world. They are strong and will always be strong. They are flexible and stretch easily. I choose the thoughts that allow me to welcome new experiences. My life is a joyous ballet. I love and appreciate my beautiful muscles!

i love my skin

My individuality is safe. The past is forgiven and forgotten. I am free and safe in this moment. I choose the thoughts that create joy and peace for myself. My skin is youthful and smooth on every part of my body. I love to caress my skin. My cells have eternal youth. My skin is the mantle that protects the temple I live in. I love and appreciate my beautiful skin!

PERSONAL NOTES ✢ AFFIRMATIONS

i love my height

I am the perfect height for me. I am neither too tall nor too short. I can look up and I can look down. I can reach for the stars and touch the earth. I choose the thoughts that enable me to always feel safe and secure and loved. I love and appreciate my beautiful height!

PERSONAL NOTES ✢ AFFIRMATIONS

i love my weight

I am the perfect weight for myself at this moment. It is exactly the weight that I have accepted for myself. I have the ability to change my weight if I desire. I choose the thoughts that keep me comfortable and satisfied with my body and its size. I love and appreciate my beautiful weight!

i love my appearance

I love my appearance. It suits me perfectly for this lifetime. I chose my looks before I was born, and I am satisfied with my choice. I am unique and special. No one else looks exactly as I do. I am beautiful, and I become more attractive every day. I choose the thoughts that give forth a beautiful appearance. I love the way I look. I love and appreciate my beautiful appearance!

PERSONAL NOTES ✣ AFFIRMATIONS

i love my age

I am the perfect age. Each year is special and precious to me for I shall only live it once. Every year from infancy to old age is filled with wonders all its own. Just as childhood is very special, so is being elderly. I want to experience it all. I choose the thoughts that make me comfortable with growing older. I look forward to each new year as it unfolds before me. I love and appreciate my beautiful age!

PERSONAL NOTES ✣ AFFIRMATIONS

i love my body

My body is a glorious place to live. I rejoice that I have chosen this particular body because it is perfect for me in this lifetime. It is the perfect size and shape and color. It serves me so well. I marvel at the miracle that is my body. I choose the healing thoughts that create and maintain my healthy body and make me feel good. I love and appreciate my beautiful body!

PERSONAL NOTES ✣ AFFIRMATIONS

Index

Holistic Healing Recommendations

Body

Getting Well Again, by O. Carl Simonton, M.D., Stephanie Matthews-Simonton, and James L. Creighton

The Great American Cookbook, by Marilyn Diamond

Healthy Healing, by Linda Page Rector

Love, Medicine & Miracles, by Bernie Siegel, M.D.

Women's Bodies, Women's Wisdom, by Christiane Northrup, M.D.

Mind

Anatomy of the Spirit, by Caroline Myss

Awakening Intuition, by Mona Lisa Schulz, M.D., Ph.D.

Feel the Fear and Do It Anyway, by Susan Jeffers, Ph.D.

"I'd Change My Life If I Had More Time," by Doreen Virtue

New Passages: Mapping Your Life Across Time, by Gail Sheehy

Women Who Love Too Much, by Robin Norwood

Spirit

Autobiography of a Yogi, by Paramahansa Yogananda

A Course in Miracles, by Foundation for Inner Peace

"I Come As a Brother," by Bartholomew

A Woman's Worth, by Marianne Williamson

Your Sacred Self, by Dr. Wayne W. Dyer

About the Author

Louise Hay, the author of the international bestseller *You Can Heal Your Life,* is a metaphysical lecturer and teacher with more than 50 million books sold worldwide. For more than 30 years, Louise has helped people throughout the world discover and implement the full potential of their own creative powers for personal growth and self-healing. She has appeared on *The Oprah Winfrey Show* and many other TV and radio programs both in the U.S. and abroad.

Websites: www.LouiseHay.com® and www.HealYourLife.com®

Hay House Titles of Related Interest

YOU CAN HEAL YOUR LIFE, the movie,
starring Louise Hay & Friends
(available as a 1-DVD program and
an expanded 2-DVD set)
Watch the trailer at: www.LouiseHayMovie.com

THE SHIFT, the movie,
starring Dr. Wayne W. Dyer
(available as a 1-DVD program and
an expanded 2-DVD set)
Watch the trailer at: www.DyerMovie.com

❖

*ASSERTIVENESS FOR EARTH ANGELS: How to Be Loving
Instead of "Too Nice,"* by Doreen Virtue

*E-SQUARED: Nine Do-It-Yourself Energy Experiments That
Prove Your Thoughts Create Your Reality,* by Pam Grout

I CAN SEE CLEARLY NOW, by Dr. Wayne W. Dyer

LOVEABILITY: Knowing How to Love and Be Loved,
by Robert Holden, Ph.D.

*NURTURING HEALING LOVE: A Mother's Journey
of Hope and Forgiveness,* by Scarlett Lewis

All of the above are available at your local bookstore,
or may be ordered by contacting Hay House (see next page).

❖

We hope you enjoyed this Hay House book. If you'd like
to receive our online catalog featuring additional information
on Hay House books and products, or if you'd like to find
out more about the Hay Foundation, please contact:

Hay House, Inc., P.O. Box 5100, Carlsbad, CA 92018-5100
(760) 431-7695 or (800) 654-5126
(760) 431-6948 (fax) or (800) 650-5115 (fax)
www.hayhouse.com® • www.hayfoundation.org

✜

Published and distributed in Australia by: Hay House
Australia Pty. Ltd., 18/36 Ralph St., Alexandria NSW 2015
Phone: 612-9669-4299 • *Fax:* 612-9669-4144 • www.hayhouse.com.au

Published and distributed in the United Kingdom by:
Hay House UK, Ltd., Astley House, 33 Notting Hill Gate,
London W11 3JQ • *Phone:* 44-20-3675-2450
Fax: 44-20-3675-2451 • www.hayhouse.co.uk

Published and distributed in the Republic of South Africa by:
Hay House SA (Pty), Ltd., P.O. Box 990, Witkoppen 2068
Phone/Fax: 27-11-467-8904 • www.hayhouse.co.za

Published in India by: Hay House Publishers India, Muskaan
Complex, Plot No. 3, B-2, Vasant Kunj, New Delhi 110 070
Phone: 91-11-4176-1620 • *Fax:* 91-11-4176-1630 • www.hayhouse.co.in

Distributed in Canada by: Raincoast Books, 2440 Viking Way,
Richmond, B.C. V6V 1N2 • *Phone:* 1-800-663-5714
Fax: 1-800-565-3770 • www.raincoast.com

✜

Take Your Soul on a Vacation

Visit www.HealYourLife.com® to regroup, recharge,
and reconnect with your own magnificence.
Featuring blogs, mind-body-spirit news, and life-
changing wisdom from Louise Hay and friends.

Visit www.HealYourLife.com today!

CPSIA information can be obtained
at www.ICGtesting.com
Printed in the USA
FSOW02n2330040417
32720FS